Are We There Yet?

Written by Jillian Powell
Illustrated by Stefania Colnaghi

WAYLAND

Rosie went for a train ride.

Her doll, Molly May,
went too.

"Is it far to the sea?"
Rosie said.

"Not far," Dad said.

Rosie read her comic.

It didn't take long.

Then Rosie did a drawing.
It didn't take long.

"Are we there yet?"
Rosie said.

"No!" Mum said.
"Here's a puzzle to do."

So Rosie did her puzzle.

It didn't take long.

"Are we there yet?"
she said again.

"No!" Dad said.

Tom came over.

"Hello, I'm Tom," he said.
"Will you play I spy...?"

Rosie and Tom played
I spy...

"I spy with my little eye
something beginning with c,"
Rosie said.

"Cows!" shouted Tom.

"My turn now," Tom said.

"I spy with my little eye something beginning with s."

Rosie jumped up and down.

"The sea! I can see
the sea!" she said.
"We're here!"

Mum, Dad and Rosie got
off the train.

"Oh no! Where's Molly
May?" Rosie said.

"Rosie, here's Molly May!"
Tom shouted.

"She wants to see the sea, too!"

START READING is a series of highly enjoyable books for beginner readers. They have been carefully graded to match the Book Bands widely used in schools. This enables readers to be sure they choose books that match their own reading ability.

The Bands are:

| Pink / Band 1 |
| Red / Band 2 |
| Yellow / Band 3 |
| Blue / Band 4 |
| Green / Band 5 |
| Orange / Band 6 |
| Turquoise / Band 7 |
| |
| Gold / Band 9 |

START READING books can be read independently or shared with an adult. They promote the enjoyment of reading through satisfying stories supported by fun illustrations.

Jillian Powell started writing stories when she was four years old. She has written many books for children, including stories about cats, dogs, scarecrows and ghosts.

Stefania Colnaghi lives with her husband in a small village near Pavia, in northern Italy. She loves drawing animals and naughty children and, in her free time, enjoys walking in the hills around her home with her dogs.

"She wants to see
the sea, too!"

START READING is a series of highly enjoyable books for beginner readers. They have been carefully graded to match the Book Bands widely used in schools. This enables readers to be sure they choose books that match their own reading ability.

The Bands are:

Pink / Band 1
Red / Band 2
Yellow / Band 3
Blue / Band 4
Green / Band 5
Orange / Band 6
Turquoise / Band 7
Purple / Band 8
Gold / Band 9

START READING books can be read independently or shared with an adult. They promote the enjoyment of reading through satisfying stories supported by fun illustrations.

Jillian Powell started writing stories when she was four years old. She has written many books for children, including stories about cats, dogs, scarecrows and ghosts.

Stefania Colnaghi lives with her husband in a small village near Pavia, in northern Italy. She loves drawing animals and naughty children and, in her free time, enjoys walking in the hills around her home with her dogs.